STEP-BY-STEP

Wok Cooking

Wok Cooking

ROSEMARY WADEY

||| •PARRAGON• |||

First published in Great Britain in 1994 by
Parragon Book Service Ltd
Unit 13-17, Avonbridge Trading Estate
Atlantic Road
Avonmouth
Bristol BS11 9QD

© Parragon Book Service Ltd 1994

ISBN 1 85813 649 0

Printed in Italy

Acknowledgements:

Design & DTP: Pedro & Frances Prá-Lopez / Kingfisher Design
Art Direction: Clive Hayball
Managing Editor: Alexa Stace
Photography: Martin Brigdale
Home Economist: Jill Eggleton
Stylist: Helen Trent
Step-by-Step Photography: Karl Adamson
Step-by-Step Home Economist: Joanna Craig

Photographs on pages 6, 18, 32, 46 & 58: By courtesy of ZEFA

Note:
Cup measurements in this book are for American cups. Tablespoons are assumed to be 15ml.

Contents

CHAPTER ONE

Soups

Traditionally, soups are carefully prepared and given plenty of time to cook. They are then often puréed to give a smooth finished dish. When using a wok the result is quick and delicious, providing ideas for soups with a difference. You can use poultry, vegetables, fish, shellfish, eggs, pasta, rice, tofu and many other ingredients to create a wide range of different soups, all attractive, colourful and well worth trying.

Preparation of the ingredients is all-important, and the actual method of cutting should be followed carefully both to ensure they are properly cooked and to give an attractive finish to the soup.

The better the stock you use the better the flavour of the soup will be. However, when homemade stock is unavailable, bought stock cubes can be used very successfully, but watch the salt content, particularly when soy sauce is also included in the recipe – always taste before adding any extra salt.

Opposite: *Fishing boats moored at dusk off Kata Beach, Thailand. The Thais are adept at wok cooking: snack meals of soup, fish or vegetables are often quickly prepared over an open fire on the beach.*

STEP 1

STEP 2

STEP 3

STEP 4

CHICKEN & SWEETCORN SOUP

A hint of chilli and sherry flavour this chicken and sweetcorn soup which has both baby sweetcorn and corn niblets in it, with red (bell) pepper and tomato for colour and flavour.

SERVES 4

1 boneless, skinned chicken breast, about 175 g/6 oz
2 tbsp sunflower oil
2-3 spring onions (scallions), thinly sliced diagonally
1 small or ½ large red (bell) pepper, cored, seeded and thinly sliced
1 garlic clove, crushed
125 g/4 oz baby sweetcorn, thinly sliced
1 litre/1¼ pints/4 cups chicken stock
1 x 200 g/7 oz can sweetcorn niblets, well drained
2 tbsp sherry
2-3 tsp bottled sweet chilli sauce
2-3 tsp cornflour (cornstarch)
2 tomatoes, peeled, quartered and seeded, then sliced
salt and pepper
freshly chopped coriander or parsley, to garnish

1 Cut the chicken breast into 4 strips lengthways, then cut each strip into narrow slices across the grain.

2 Heat the oil in a wok, swirling it around until it is really hot. Add the chicken and stir-fry for 3-4 minutes, spreading it out over the wok until it is well sealed all over and almost cooked.

3 Add the spring onions (scallions), (bell) pepper and garlic and continue to stir-fry for 2-3 minutes, then add the baby sweetcorns and stock and bring to the boil.

4 Add the corn niblets, sherry and sweet chilli sauce and salt to taste and simmer for 5 minutes, stirring from time to time.

5 Blend the cornflour (cornstarch) with a little cold water, add to the soup and bring to the boil. Add the strips of tomato, adjust the seasoning and simmer for a few minutes. Serve the soup very hot, sprinkled with finely chopped coriander or parsley.

VARIATION

This soup may be flavoured with curry instead of chilli for a change. Omit the sherry and chilli sauce and add ½-1 teaspoon medium curry powder and ½ teaspoon garam masala while stir-frying the chicken.

FISH & VEGETABLE SOUP

A chunky fish soup with strips of vegetables, all flavoured with ginger and lemon, makes a meal in itself.

STEP 1

SERVES 4

250 g/8 oz white fish fillets (cod, halibut, haddock, sole etc)
½ tsp ground ginger
½ tsp salt
1 small leek, trimmed
2-4 crab sticks, defrosted if frozen (optional)
1 tbsp sunflower oil
1 large carrot, cut into julienne strips
8 canned water chestnuts, thinly sliced
1.25 litres/2 pints/5 cups fish or vegetable stock
1 tbsp lemon juice
1 tbsp light soy sauce
1 large courgette (zucchini), cut into julienne strips
black pepper

1 Remove any skin from the fish and cut into cubes, about 2.5 cm/1 in. Combine the ground ginger and salt and use to rub into the pieces of fish. Leave to marinate for at least 30 minutes.

2 Meanwhile, divide the green and white parts of the leek. Cut each part into 2.5 cm/1 in lengths and then into julienne strips down the length of each piece, keeping the two parts separate. Slice the crab sticks into 1 cm/½ in pieces.

3 Heat the oil in the wok, swirling it around so it is really hot. Add the white part of the leek and stir-fry for a couple of minutes, then add the carrots and water chestnuts and continue to cook for 1-2 minutes, stirring thoroughly.

4 Add the stock and bring to the boil, then add the lemon juice and soy sauce and simmer for 2 minutes.

5 Add the fish and continue to cook for about 5 minutes until the fish begins to break up a little, then add the green part of the leek and the courgettes (zucchini) and simmer for about 1 minute. Add the sliced crab sticks, if using, and season to taste with black pepper. Simmer for a further minute or so and serve piping hot.

STEP 2

STEP 3

STEP 5

STEP 1

STEP 2a

STEP 2b

STEP 3

CHICKEN SOUP WITH ALMONDS

This soup can also be made using turkey or pheasant breasts. Pheasant gives a stronger, gamy flavour, particularly if game stock is made from the carcass and used in the soup.

SERVES 4

1 large or 2 small boneless skinned chicken
   breasts
1 tbsp sunflower oil
4 spring onions (scallions), thinly sliced
   diagonally
1 carrot, cut into julienne strips
750 ml/ 1¼ pints/ 3 cups chicken stock
finely grated rind of ½ lemon
45 g/ 1½ oz/ ⅓ cup ground almonds
1 tbsp light soy sauce
1 tbsp lemon juice
30 g/ 1 oz/ ¼ cup flaked almonds, toasted
salt and pepper

1 Cut each breast into 4 strips lengthways, then slice very thinly across the grain to give shreds of chicken.

2 Heat the oil in the wok, swirling it around until really hot. Add the chicken and toss it for 3-4 minutes until sealed and almost cooked through, then add the carrot and continue to cook for 2-3 minutes, stirring all the time. Add the spring onions (scallions) and stir.

3 Add the stock to the wok and bring to the boil. Add the lemon rind, ground almonds, soy sauce, lemon juice and plenty of seasoning. Bring back to the boil and simmer, uncovered, for 5 minutes, stirring from time to time.

4 Adjust the seasoning, add most of the toasted flaked almonds and continue to cook for a further 1-2 minutes.

5 Serve the soup very hot, in individual bowls, sprinkled with the remaining almonds.

GAME STOCK

To make game stock, break up a pheasant carcass and place in a large pan with 2 litres/3½ pints/8 cups of water. Bring to the boil slowly, skimming off the scum as it rises to the surface. Add 1 bouquet garni, 1 small onion, peeled, and salt and pepper. Cover and simmer gently for about 1½ hours, skimming regularly. Strain the stock and skim any fat off the surface. Makes about 1.25 litres/2 pints/ 5 cups.

PRAWN (SHRIMP) SOUP

*A mixture of textures and flavours make this an interesting and
colourful soup. The egg may be made into a flat omelette
and added as thin strips if preferred.*

STEP 1

SERVES 4

2 tbsp sunflower oil
2 spring onions (scallions), thinly sliced
   diagonally
1 carrot, coarsely grated
125 g/4 oz large closed cup mushrooms,
   thinly sliced
1 litre/1¾ pints/4 cups fish or vegetable
   stock
½ tsp Chinese five-spice powder
1 tbsp light soy sauce
125 g/4 oz large peeled prawns (shrimp) or
   peeled tiger prawns (shrimp), defrosted if
   frozen
½ bunch of watercress, trimmed and
   roughly chopped
1 egg, well beaten
salt and pepper
4 large prawns (shrimp) in shells, to
   garnish (optional)

1 Heat the oil in a wok, swirling it
around until really hot. Add the
spring onions (scallions) and stir-fry for a
minute then add the carrots and
mushrooms and continue to cook for
about 2 minutes.

2 Add the stock and bring up to the
boil then season to taste with salt
and pepper, five-spice powder and soy

STEP 2a

sauce and simmer for 5 minutes.
If the prawns (shrimp) are really large,
cut them in half before adding to the wok
and then continue to simmer for 3-4
minutes.

3 Add the roughly chopped
watercress to the wok and mix
well, then slowly pour in the beaten egg
in a circular movement so that it cooks in
threads in the soup.

4 Adjust the seasoning and serve
each portion topped with a whole
prawn (shrimp).

step 2b

MUSHROOMS

The large open mushrooms with black
gills give the best flavour but they tend to
spoil the colour of the soup, making it very
dark. Oyster mushrooms can also be used.

STEP 3

15

SPINACH & TOFU SOUP

Tofu (bean curd) is very popular with non-meat-eaters, being a good source of protein.

STEP 1

SERVES 4

125-175 g/4-6 oz fresh spinach leaves, or
   frozen leaf spinach, defrosted
small bunch of chives
2 tbsp sesame oil
1 garlic clove, crushed
125-175 g/4-6 oz tofu (bean curd), cut
   into 1 cm/$^1\!/_2$ in cubes
60 g/2 oz/$^1\!/_2$ cup pine kernels
1 litre/1$^3\!/_4$ pints/4 cups good chicken or
   vegetable stock
$^1\!/_2$ tsp turmeric
$^1\!/_2$ tsp ground coriander
2 tsp cornflour (cornstarch)
salt and pepper

1 Wash the spinach thoroughly and strip off the stalks. Dry on paper towels, then slice into thin strips. If using frozen spinach, drain well, then slice or chop roughly.

2 Take 12 chives and tie 3 at a time into a knot to use for a garnish, if liked. Chop the remainder.

3 Heat the oil in a wok, swirling it around until really hot. Add the garlic and tofu and stir-fry for 2-3 minutes until they are beginning to colour. Add the pine kernels and

continue to cook until they turn a light golden brown.

4 Add the stock, turmeric, coriander and seasoning and bring to the boil; simmer for 10 minutes.

5 Blend the cornflour (cornstarch) with a little cold water and stir into the wok. Add the strips of spinach and simmer for a further 2-3 minutes, stirring frequently.

6 Adjust the seasoning, stir in the snipped chives and garnish each serving with a chive knot, if liked.

STEP 3

STEP 4

TOFU (BEAN CURD)

Tofu can be added to many dishes – soups, stir-fries or vegetable stews – to provide extra protein. It is very bland and almost tasteless, so some extra flavouring is usually required.

STEP 5

CHAPTER TWO

Fish

Both fish and shellfish lend themselves beautifully to cooking in a wok. Fish keeps its shape, texture and maximum flavour when cooked in a wok and a wide variety of flavourings – such as herbs, spices and prepared vegetables – can be added to ring the changes. Select firm-textured fish such as monkfish, halibut, sole, salmon or cod: skin and cut into even-sized pieces, ready to stir-fry or shallow-fry. You can also cook large juicy prawns (shrimp), peeled. Large mussels and other pieces of shellfish can be coated in batter, egg and crumbs, coconut, sesame seeds etc, and deep-fried or shallow-fried. Try steaming fish steaks, fillets or strips of fish in the bamboo steamer along with shellfish such as prawns, mussels and scallops, which all benefit from this light and gentle method of cooking. You can even try cooking mussels in a wok to give the old favourite Moules Marinière a new dimension: steam or braise the mussels in a wine sauce flavoured with onion, garlic, herbs and butter. The size and shape of the wok help immensely with the stirring and mixing of the mussels, and the extra heat distribution speeds up a dish which is already quick to cook.

Opposite: *A dried fish stall in Macau. Nothing is wasted in oriental cooking, and surplus fish are dried to provide a valuable source of protein. Tiny dried shrimps are widely used as a flavouring in soups and sauces.*

STEP 1

STEP 2

STEP 3

STEP 4

PRAWNS (SHRIMP) IN SAUCE

Use raw tiger prawns (shrimp) with the shell removed and just the tail left in place. If frozen, make sure they are well defrosted, and dry thoroughly on paper towels to prevent excess spluttering in the hot oil.

SERVES 4

20-24 large raw tiger prawns (shrimp)
45 g/1¹/₂ oz/¹/₂ cup desiccated (shredded)
    coconut
90 g/3 oz/1¹/₂ cups fresh white
    breadcrumbs
1 egg, beaten
600 ml/1 pint/2¹/₂ cups sunflower or
    vegetable oil
fresh sprigs of coriander, to garnish

PEANUT AND COCONUT SAUCE:
60 g/2 oz creamed coconut
150 ml/¹/₄ pint/²/₃ cup hot water
125 g/4 oz crunchy peanut butter
2 spring onions (scallions), trimmed and
    finely chopped
1 tbsp dark soy sauce
1 tsp brown sugar
2 tsp sesame seeds
salt and pepper
¹/₂ small Ogen or charentais melon

1 Peel the tiger prawns (shrimp), leaving the tails, and dry thoroughly on paper towels. Put the coconut and breadcrumbs into a food processor and process until well blended and chopped finely. Spread the coconut mixture on a plate. Dip the prawns (shrimp) in the beaten egg then coat thoroughly in the coconut and breadcrumb mixture. Chill while making the sauce.

2 For the sauce, put the creamed coconut and water into the wok and blend thoroughly, then bring slowly up to the boil. Remove from the heat, stir in the peanut butter, spring onions (scallions), soy sauce, sugar, sesame seeds and seasoning and when blended put into a serving bowl and keep warm.

3 Cut the melon into 12 slices, removing the seeds.

4 Wash and dry the wok, add the oil and heat to 180°-190°C/350°-375°F, or until a cube of bread browns in 30 seconds. Deep-fry the prawns (shrimp) a few at a time for 2-3 minutes until golden brown. Remove with a slotted spoon and drain on paper towels. Keep warm while cooking the remainder.

5 Serve immediately on individual plates, with slices of melon, garnished with sprigs of coriander. Serve the warm sauce in its bowl.

STEP 1a

STEP 1b

STEP 2a

STEP 2b

SOLE PAUPIETTES

A delicate dish of sole fillets rolled up with spinach and prawns, (shrimp), and served in a creamy ginger sauce.

---

125 g/4 oz fresh young spinach leaves
2 Dover soles or large lemon soles or plaice,
*   filleted*
125 g/4 oz peeled prawns (shrimp),
*   defrosted if frozen*
2 tsp sunflower oil
2-4 spring onions (scallions), finely sliced
*   diagonally*
2 thin slices ginger root, finely chopped
150 ml/¹/₄ pint/²/₃ cup fish stock or water
2 tsp cornflour (cornstarch)
4 tbsp single cream
6 tbsp natural yogurt
salt and pepper
whole prawns (shrimp), to garnish
*   (optional)*

1 Strip the stalks off the spinach, wash and dry on paper towels. Divide the spinach between the seasoned fish fillets, laying the leaves on the skin side. Divide half the prawns (shrimp) between them. Roll up the fillets from head to tail and secure with wooden cocktail sticks. Arrange the rolls on a plate in the base of a bamboo steamer.

2 Stand a low metal trivet in the wok and add enough water to come almost to the top of it. Bring to the boil. Place the bamboo steamer on the trivet, cover with the steamer lid and then the

wok lid, or cover tightly with a domed piece of foil. Steam gently for 30 minutes until the fish is tender and cooked through.

3 Remove the fish rolls and keep warm. Empty the wok and wipe dry. Heat the oil in the wok, swirling it around until really hot. Add the spring onions (scallions) and ginger and stir-fry for 1-2 minutes. Add the stock and bring to the boil.

4 Blend the cornflour (cornstarch) with the cream. Add the yogurt and remaining prawns (shrimp) to the wok and heat gently until boiling. Add a little sauce to the blended cream and return it all to the wok. Heat gently until thickened. Adjust the seasoning. Serve the paupiettes with the sauce spooned over and garnished with whole prawns (shrimp), if liked.

BAJAN FISH

Bajan seasoning comes from Barbados and can be used with all kinds of meat, fish, poultry and game. Add more chilli if you like it really hot.

STEP 2

SERVES 4

500-625 g / 1-1¼ lb monkfish tails, boned and cubed
2 large carrots
175-250 g/6-8 oz baby sweetcorn
3 tbsp sunflower oil
1 courgette (zucchini), sliced
1 yellow (bell) pepper, cored, seeded and thinly sliced
1 tbsp wine vinegar
150 ml/¼ pint/⅔ cup fish or vegetable stock
1 tbsp lemon juice
2 tbsp sherry
1 tsp cornflour (cornstarch)
salt and pepper
fresh herbs and lemon slices, to garnish

BAJAN SEASONING:
1 small onion, quartered
2 shallots
3-4 garlic cloves, crushed
4-6 large spring onions (scallions), sliced
small handful of fresh parsley
2-3 sprigs of fresh thyme
small strip of green chilli pepper, seeds removed, or ½-¼ tsp chilli powder
½ tsp salt
¼ tsp freshly ground black pepper
2 tbsp brown rum or red wine vinegar

1 First make the Bajan seasoning. Place all the ingredients in a food processor and process very finely.

2 Put the fish in a shallow dish and spread the Bajan seasoning over it, turning to coat evenly. Cover with clingfilm and leave to marinate for at least 30 minutes and up to 24 hours.

3 Cut the carrots into narrow 4 cm/1½ in slices and slice the baby sweetcorn diagonally.

4 Heat 2 tablespoons of oil in the wok, swirling it around until really hot. Add the fish and stir-fry for 3-4 minutes until cooked through. Remove to a bowl and keep warm.

5 Add the remaining oil to the wok and when hot stir-fry the carrots and corn for 2 minutes, then add the (bell) pepper and stir-fry for another minute or so. Return the fish and juices to the wok and stir-fry for 1-2 minutes.

6 Blend the vinegar, stock, lemon juice, sherry and seasoning with the cornflour (cornstarch). Stir into the wok and boil until the sauce thickens. Serve garnished with herbs and lemon.

STEP 4

STEP 5

STEP 6

STEP 1

STEP 2

STEP 3

STEP 4

SPICED SCALLOPS

Scallops are available both fresh and frozen. Make sure they are completely defrosted before cooking.

SERVES 4

12 large scallops with coral attached, defrosted if frozen, or 350 g/12 oz small scallops without coral, defrosted
4 tbsp sunflower oil
4-6 spring onions (scallions), thinly sliced diagonally
1 garlic clove, crushed
2.5 cm/1 in ginger root, finely chopped
250 g/8 oz mangetout (snow peas)
125 g/4 oz button or closed cup mushrooms, sliced
2 tbsp sherry
2 tbsp soy sauce
1 tbsp clear honey
1/4 tsp ground allspice
salt and pepper
1 tbsp sesame seeds, toasted

1 Wash and dry the scallops, discarding any black pieces and detach the corals, if using. Slice each scallop into 3-4 pieces and if the corals are large halve them.

2 Heat 2 tablespoons of oil in the wok, swirling it around until really hot. Add the spring onions (scallions), garlic and ginger and stir-fry for a minute or so then add the mangetout (snow peas) and continue to cook for 2-3

minutes, stirring continuously. Remove to a bowl.

3 Add the remaining oil to the wok and when really hot add the scallops and corals and stir-fry for a couple of minutes. Add the mushrooms and continue to cook for a further minute or so.

4 Add the sherry, soy sauce, honey and allspice to the wok, with salt and pepper to taste. Mix thoroughly, then return the mangetout (snow peas) mixture to the wok.

5 Season well and toss together over a high heat for a minute or so until piping hot. Serve immediately, sprinkled with sesame seeds.

SCALLOPS ON THE SHELL

If you buy scallops on the shell, slide a knife underneath the membrane to loosen and cut off the tough muscle that holds the scallop to the shell. Discard the black stomach sac and intestinal vein.

STEP 1

STEP 2

STEP 5

STEP 6

FISH WITH SAFFRON SAUCE

White fish cooked in a bamboo steamer over the wok and served with a light creamy saffron sauce with a real bite to it.

SERVES 4

625-750 g/1¼-1½ lb white fish fillets
   (cod, haddock, whiting etc)
pinch of Chinese five-spice powder
4 sprigs of fresh thyme
large pinch of saffron threads
250 ml/8 fl oz/1 cup boiling fish or
   vegetable stock
2 tbsp sunflower oil
125 g/4 oz button mushrooms, thinly sliced
grated rind of ½ lemon
1 tbsp lemon juice
½ tsp freshly chopped thyme or ¼ tsp dried
   thyme
½ bunch watercress, chopped
1½ tsp cornflour
3 tbsp single or double (heavy) cream
salt and pepper
lemon and watercress sprigs, to garnish

1 Skin the fish and cut into 4 even-sized portions. Season with salt and pepper and five-spice powder. Arrange the fish on a plate and place in the bottom of a bamboo steamer, laying a sprig of thyme on each piece of fish (if the fillets are large you may need 2 steamers, one on top of the other).

2 Stand a low metal trivet in a wok and add water to come almost to the top of it. Bring to the boil, stand the bamboo steamer on the trivet and cover with first the bamboo lid and then the lid of the wok. If there is no wok lid, make one out of a domed piece of foil pressed tightly to the sides of the wok. Simmer for about 20 minutes until the fish is tender, adding more boiling water to the wok as necessary.

3 Meanwhile, soak the saffron threads in the boiling stock.

4 When the fish is tender, remove and keep warm. Empty the wok and wipe dry. Heat the oil in the wok, add the mushrooms and stir-fry for about 2 minutes.

5 Add the saffron stock, lemon rind and juice and chopped thyme and bring to the boil. Add the watercress and simmer for a 1-2 minutes.

6 Blend the cornflour with the cream, add a little of the sauce from the wok, mix well, then return to the wok and heat gently until thickened. Remove the sprigs of thyme from the fish and serve surrounded by the sauce with a little spooned over it and garnished with lemon and watercress.

STEP 1

STEP 2

STEP 3

STEP 4

SESAME SALMON & CREAM SAUCE

Salmon fillet holds its shape when tossed in sesame seeds and stir-fried. It is served in a creamy sauce of diced courgettes (zucchini) flavoured with turmeric.

SERVES 4

625-750 g / 1¼ - 1½ lb salmon or pink trout fillets
2 tbsp light soy sauce
3 tbsp sesame seeds
3 tbsp sunflower oil
4 spring onions (scallions), thinly sliced diagonally
2 large courgettes (zucchini), diced, or 2.5 cm / 5 in piece of cucumber, diced
grated rind of ½ lemon
½ tsp turmeric
1 tbsp lemon juice
6 tbsp fish stock or water
3 tbsp double (heavy) cream or fromage frais
salt and pepper
curly endive, to garnish

1 Skin the salmon and cut into strips about 4 x 2 cm / 1½ x ¾ in. Pat dry on paper towels. Season lightly, then brush with soy sauce and sprinkle all over with sesame seeds.

2 Heat 2 tablespoons of oil in the wok, swirling it around until really hot. Add the pieces of salmon and stir-fry for 3-4 minutes until lightly browned all over. Remove with a fish slice, drain on paper towels and keep warm.

3 Add the remaining oil to the wok and when hot add the spring onions (scallions) and courgettes (zucchini) or cucumber and stir-fry for 1-2 minutes. Add the lemon rind and juice, turmeric, stock and seasoning and bring to the boil for a minute or so. Stir the cream or fromage frais into the sauce.

4 Return the salmon pieces to the wok and toss gently in the sauce until they are really hot. Serve on warm plates and garnish with curly endive, if using.

SKINNING FISH

Lay the fillet skin-side down. Insert a sharp, flexible knife at one end between the flesh and the skin. Hold the skin tightly at the end and push the knife along, keeping the knife blade as flat as possible against the skin.

CHAPTER THREE

Vegetables

Fresh vegetables are at their best when served still crisp and full of flavour. Once they are over-cooked and soggy everything is lost – nutrients, texture, flavour and appearance. With the wok it is easy to serve vegetables at their best at all times.

It is important that the produce used is in prime condition: the wok will only enhance the flavour and texture of fresh foods: it cannot improve poor quality ingredients. It is also important to prepare the vegetables before you begin to cook: make sure they are cut into even-sized pieces and shapes with the maximum amount of exposed surface, by cutting on the diagonal or into matchsticks.

Experiment with all types of vegetables – celery, carrots, spring onions, celeriac, turnips and parsnips for root varieties, and others such as mushrooms, leeks, beans, baby sweetcorn, mangetout (sugar peas); and don't forget the canned varieties like water chestnuts, bamboo shoots and hearts of palm for texture, shape and colour.

Opposite: A producer brings his tomatoes to market in Xinjiang, China. It is important in wok cooking that vegetables are absolutely fresh – the Chinese set great store by fresh fruit and vegetables, and therefore shop daily in the market.

AVIYAL

This is a mixture of vegetables flavoured lightly with coconut, ginger and spices to give an Indian flavour. It can be served with any type of food, and also makes a good vegetarian main dish.

STEP 1

SERVES 4

250 g/ 8 oz/ 2²/₃ cups desiccated (shredded) coconut or 125 g (4 oz) creamed coconut
300 ml/ ½ pint/ 1¼ cups boiling water
2 tbsp sunflower oil
30 g/ 1 oz ginger root, grated
2 onions, finely chopped
1 garlic clove, crushed
2 green (bell) peppers, cored, seeded and sliced in thin rings
1 red or yellow (bell) pepper, cored, seeded and sliced in thin rings
2 carrots, cut into julienne strips
1 green chilli pepper, cored, seeded and sliced (optional)
125-175 g/4-6 oz French or fine beans, cut into 7 cm/ 3 in lengths
175 g/6 oz green broccoli, divided into florets
2 tsp ground coriander
1 tbsp garam masala
1 tsp turmeric
3 tomatoes, peeled, quartered and seeded
salt and pepper

1 Soak the coconut in the boiling water for 20 minutes, then process in a food processor until smooth, or blend the creamed coconut with the boiling water until smooth.

2 Heat the oil in the wok, swirling it around until really hot. Add the ginger, onions and garlic and stir-fry for 2-3 minutes until they are beginning to colour lightly.

3 Add the coriander, garam masala and turmeric and continue to stir-fry for a few minutes then add the rest of the vegetables and stir-fry for 4–5 minutes, turning the heat down a little.

4 Add the coconut purée and plenty of seasoning and bring to the boil. Continue to simmer and stir-fry for about 5–8 minutes, until tender but still with a bite to the vegetables.

5 Serve as a main dish with boiled rice or noodles, or as a curry accompaniment.

STEP 2

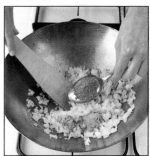

STEP 3

STEP 4

STEP 1

STEP 2

STEP 3

STEP 4

CARROTS WITH PINEAPPLE

If you can use fresh pineapple the flavour is even better and the texture crisper.

SERVES 4

1 tbsp sunflower oil
1 tbsp olive oil
1 small onion, finely sliced
2.5 cm/1 in piece ginger root, peeled and grated
1-2 garlic cloves, crushed
500 g/1 lb carrots, thinly sliced
1 x 200 g/7 oz can pineapple in natural juice, chopped, or 250 g/8 oz fresh pineapple, chopped
2-3 tbsp pineapple juice (from the can or fresh)
salt and pepper
freshly chopped parsley or dill, to garnish

1 Heat the oil in the wok, swirling it around until it is really hot. Add the onion, ginger and garlic and stir-fry briskly for 2-3 minutes, taking care not to allow it to colour.

2 Add the carrots and continue to stir-fry, lowering the heat a little, for about 5 minutes, spreading the slices out evenly over the surface of the wok as you stir.

3 Add the pineapple and juice and plenty of seasoning and continue to stir-fry for 5-6 minutes, or until the carrots are tender-crisp and the liquid has almost evaporated.

4 Adjust the seasoning, adding plenty of black pepper (the extra-coarse type is good to use here) and turn into a warmed serving dish. Sprinkle with chopped parsley or dill and serve as a vegetable accompaniment. Alternatively, you can allow the carrots to cool and serve as a salad, dressed with 2-4 tablespoons French dressing.

CANNED FRUIT

If using canned pineapple make sure it is in natural juice, not syrup: the sweet taste of the syrup will ruin the fresh flavour of this dish. Most fruits can now be bought canned in natural juice, which gives a much fresher, lighter taste.

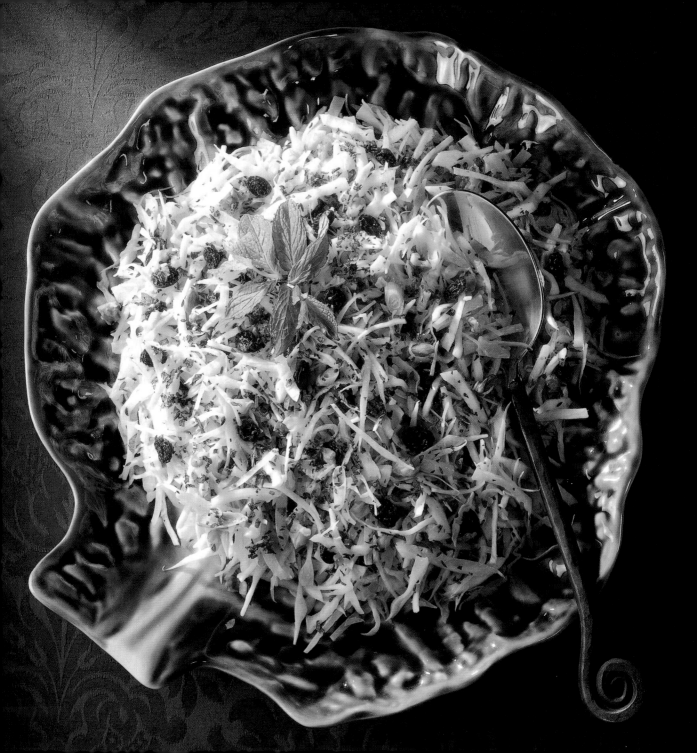

CARAWAY CABBAGE

*This makes a delicious vegetable accompaniment to all types of food:
it can also be served as a vegetarian main dish.*

STEP 1

SERVES 4

500 g/ 1 lb white cabbage
1 tbsp sunflower oil
4 spring onions (scallions), thinly sliced
    diagonally
60 g/ 2 oz/ 6 tbsp raisins
60 g/ 2 oz/ ½ cup walnut pieces or pecan
    nuts, roughly chopped
5 tbsp milk or vegetable stock
salt and pepper
1 tbsp caraway seeds
1-2 tbsp freshly chopped mint
mint sprigs, to garnish

1 Remove any outer leaves from the cabbage and cut out the stem, then shred the leaves very finely, either by hand or using the fine slicing blade on a food processor.

2 Heat the oil in a wok, swirling it around until it is really hot. Add the spring onions (scallions) and stir-fry for a minute or so.

3 Add the shredded cabbage and stir-fry for 3-4 minutes, keeping the cabbage moving all the time and stirring from the outside to the centre of the wok. Make sure the cabbage does not catch or go brown.

4 Add the raisins and walnuts and the milk and continue to stir-fry for 3-4 minutes until the cabbage begins to slightly soften but is still crisp.

5 Season well, add the caraway seeds and 1 tablespoon of the chopped mint and continue to stir-fry for a minute or so. Serve sprinkled with the remaining chopped mint and garnish with sprigs of fresh mint.

STEP 3

VARIATION

Red cabbage may be cooked in the same way in the wok, but substitute 2 tablespoons red or white wine vinegar and 3 tablespoons water for the milk and add 1 tablespoon brown sugar. The caraway seeds may be omitted if liked and a finely chopped dessert apple added with the cabbage. Replace the chopped mint with chopped parsley.

STEP 4

STEP 5

MIXED BEAN STIR-FRY

Any type of canned beans can be used – butter beans, black-eyed beans etc – but rinse under cold water and drain well before use.

STEP 2

STEP 3

STEP 4

STEP 5

SERVES 4

1 x 425 g/15 oz can red kidney beans
1 x 425 g/15 oz can cannellini beans
6 spring onions (scallions)
1 x 200 g/7 oz can pineapple rings or pieces
   in natural juice, chopped
2 tbsp pineapple juice
3-4 pieces stem ginger
2 tbsp ginger syrup from the jar
thinly pared rind of ¹/₂ lime or lemon, cut
   into julienne strips
2 tbsp lime or lemon juice
2 tbsp soy sauce
1 tsp cornflour (cornstarch)
1 tbsp sesame oil
125 g/4 oz French beans, cut into 4 cm/
   1¹/₂ in lengths
1 x 250 g/8 oz can bamboo shoots, drained
   and thinly sliced
salt and pepper

1 Drain all the beans, rinse under cold water and drain again very thoroughly.

2 Cut 4 spring onions (scallions) into narrow slanting slices. Thinly slice the remainder and reserve for garnish.

3 Combine the pineapple and juice, ginger and syrup, lime rind and

juice, soy sauce and cornflour (cornstarch) in a bowl.

4 Heat the oil in the wok, swirling it around until really hot. Add the spring onions (scallions) and stir-fry for a minute or so. Add the French beans and bamboo shoots and continue to stir-fry for 2 minutes.

5 Add the pineapple and ginger mixture and bring just to the boil. Add the canned beans and stir until very hot – about a minute or so.

6 Season to taste, and serve with freshly boiled rice sprinkled with the reserved chopped spring onions (scallions); or serve as a vegetable accompaniment.

CANNED BEANS

Be sure to drain and rinse the beans before using, as the canning liquid usually contains brine, which will spoil the flavour of the finished dish.

STEP 1

STEP 3

STEP 4

STEP 5

CHINESE HOT SALAD

A mixture of vegetables stir-fried with a Chinese flavour, with an added touch of chilli. To serve cold, add 3-4 tablespoons French dressing as it cools, toss well and serve cold or chilled.

SERVES 4

1 tbsp dark soy sauce
1½-2 tsp bottled sweet chilli sauce
2 tbsp sherry
1 tbsp brown sugar
1 tbsp wine vinegar
2 tbsp sunflower oil
1 garlic clove, crushed
4 spring onions (scallions), thinly sliced
    diagonally
250 g/8 oz courgettes (zucchini) cut into
    julienne strips about 4 cm/1½ in long
250 g/8 oz carrots, cut into julienne strips
    about 4 cm/1½ in long
1 red or green (bell) pepper, cored, seeded
    and thinly sliced
1 x 400 g/14 oz can bean-sprouts, well
    drained
125 g/4 oz French or fine beans, cut into 5
    cm/2 in lengths
1 tbsp sesame oil
salt and pepper
1-2 tsp sesame seeds, to garnish

1 Blend the soy sauce, chilli sauce, sherry, sugar, vinegar and seasonings together.

2 Heat the 2 tablespoons of sunflower oil in a wok, swirling it around until it is really hot.

3 Add the garlic and spring onions (scallions) to the wok and stir-fry for 1-2 minutes.

4 Add the courgettes (zucchini), carrots and (bell) peppers and stir-fry for 1-2 minutes, then add the soy sauce mixture and bring to the boil.

5 Add the bean-sprouts and French beans and stir-fry for 1-2 minutes, making sure all the vegetables are thoroughly coated with the sauce.

6 Drizzle the sesame oil over the vegetables in the wok, stir-fry for about 30 seconds and serve hot sprinkled with sesame seeds.

VARIATION

Other vegetables may be used in this recipe, including mushrooms, mangetout (snow peas), baby sweetcorn, broccoli etc.

SWEET & SOUR VEGETABLES

Make your own choice of vegetables from the suggested list, including spring onions (scallions) and garlic. For a hotter, spicier sauce add chilli sauce.

STEP 1

STEP 2

SERVES 4

5-6 vegetables from the following:
1 (bell) pepper, red, green or yellow, cored, seeded and sliced
125 g/4 oz French beans, cut into 2-3 pieces
125 g/4 oz mangetout (snow peas), cut into 2-3 pieces
250 g/8 oz green broccoli or cauliflower, divided into tiny florets
250 g/8 oz courgettes (zucchini), cut into thin 5 cm/2 in lengths
175 g/6 oz carrots, cut into julienne strips
125 g/4 oz baby sweetcorn, sliced thinly
2 leeks, sliced thinly and cut into matchsticks
175 g/6 oz parsnip, finely diced
175 g/6 oz celeriac, finely diced
3 celery sticks, thinly sliced crosswise
4 tomatoes, peeled, quartered and seeded
125 g/4 oz button or closed cup mushrooms, thinly sliced
7 cm/3 in length of cucumber, diced
1 x 200 g/7 oz can water chestnuts or bamboo shoots, drained and sliced
1 x 425 g/15 oz can bean-sprouts or hearts of palm, drained and sliced
4 spring onions (scallions) trimmed and thinly sliced
1 garlic clove, crushed
2 tbsp sunflower oil

SWEET & SOUR SAUCE:
2 tbsp wine vinegar
2 tbsp clear honey
1 tbsp tomato purée (paste)
2 tbsp soy sauce
2 tbsp sherry
1-2 tsp sweet chilli sauce (optional)
2 tsp cornflour (cornstarch)

1 Prepare the selected vegetables, cutting them into uniform lengths.

2 Combine the sauce ingredients in a bowl, blending well together.

3 Heat the oil in the wok, swirling it around until really hot. Add the spring onions (scallions) and garlic and stir-fry for 1 minute.

4 Add the prepared vegetables – the harder and firmer ones first – and stir-fry for 2 minutes. Then add the softer ones such as mushrooms, mangetout (snow peas) and tomatoes and continue to stir-fry for 2 minutes.

5 Add the sweet and sour mixture to the wok and bring to the boil quickly, tossing all the vegetables until they are thoroughly coated and the sauce has thickened. Serve hot.

STEP 4

STEP 5

CHAPTER FOUR

Rice

A wok is as good as any saucepan for cooking rice, and probably
better than most, especially if you use the absorption
method of cooking the rice, because of the
extra heat distribution in the wok.

It is important to measure the amount of rice and liquid very
accurately, and also to rinse the rice thoroughly under cold
running water before you begin. Flavourings and vegetables can be
cooked along with the rice: stir-fry first, before adding the
well-drained rice, followed by the liquid. Alternatively, you can add
cooked vegetables at the end. A tightly-fitting lid is essential
to keep in the steam which helps to cook the rice; and when the
cooking time is up, all that is necessary is
to fork up the rice and serve it.

Fried rice is also at its best when cooked in a wok. The rice must be
cooked first and then allowed to cool and dry before commencing
the next stage. The omelette served with it can also be made
in the wok, and when the whole dish is put together,
the unique shape of the wok makes it so
much easier to stir the ingredients together
for a really professional-looking result.

Opposite: *Planting rice in
India. Rice is grown all over
South-East Asia and is still
planted in the traditional
labour-intensive way.*

47

NASI GORENG

An Indonesian rice dish flavoured with vegetables and pork, soy sauce and curry spices with strips of omelette added as a topping.

STEP 2

SERVES 4

300 g/10 oz/1½ cups long-grain rice
350-500 g/12 oz-1 lb pork fillet or lean
   pork slices
3 tomatoes, peeled, quartered and seeded
2 eggs
4 tsp water
3 tbsp sunflower oil
1 onion, thinly sliced
1-2 garlic cloves, crushed
1 tsp medium or mild curry powder
½ tsp ground coriander
¼ tsp medium chilli powder or 1 tsp bottled
   sweet chilli sauce
2 tbsp soy sauce
125 g/4 oz frozen peas, defrosted
salt and pepper

1 Cook the rice in boiling salted water, following the instructions given in Chinese Fried Rice (see page 56) and keep warm.

2 Meanwhile, cut the pork into narrow strips across the grain, discarding any fat. Slice the tomatoes.

3 Beat each egg separately with 2 teaspoons cold water and salt and pepper. Heat 2 teaspoons of oil in the wok, swirling it around until really hot.

4 Pour in the first egg, swirl it around and cook undisturbed until set. Remove to a plate or board and repeat with the second egg. Cut the omelettes into strips about 1 cm/½ in wide.

5 Heat the remaining oil in the wok and when really hot add the onion and garlic and stir-fry for 1-2 minutes. Add the pork and continue to stir-fry for about 3 minutes or until almost cooked.

6 Add the curry powder, coriander, chilli powder or chilli sauce and soy sauce to the wok and cook for a further minute, stirring constantly.

7 Stir in the rice, tomatoes and peas and stir-fry for about 2 minutes until piping hot. Adjust the seasoning and turn into a heated serving dish. Arrange the strips of omelette on top and serve at once.

STEP 4

STEP 5

STEP 7

STEP 2

STEP 3

STEP 4

STEP 5

RICE WITH CRAB & MUSSELS

Shellfish makes an ideal partner for rice. Mussels and crab add flavour and texture to this spicy dish.

SERVES 4, OR 6 AS A STARTER

300 g / 10 oz / 1½ cups long-grain rice
175 g / 6 oz crab meat, fresh, canned or
*   frozen (defrosted if frozen), or 8 crab*
*   sticks, defrosted if frozen*
2 tbsp sesame or sunflower oil
2.5 cm / 1 in ginger root, grated
4 spring onions (scallions), thinly sliced
*   diagonally*
125 g / 4 oz mangetout (snow peas), cut into
*   2-3 pieces*
½ tsp turmeric
1 tsp ground cumin
2 x 200 g / 7 oz jars mussels, well drained,
*   or 350 g / 12 oz frozen mussels, defrosted*
1 x 425 g / 15 oz can bean-sprouts, well
*   drained*
salt and pepper

TO GARNISH:
crab claws or legs (optional)
8 mangetout (snow peas), blanched

1 Cook the rice in boiling salted water, following the instructions given in Chinese Fried Rice (see page 56).

2 Meanwhile, extract the crab meat, if using fresh crab (see right). Flake the crab meat or cut the crab sticks into 3 or 4 pieces.

3 Heat the oil in the wok, swirling it around until really hot. Add the ginger and spring onions (scallions) and stir-fry for a minute or so. Add the mangetout (snow peas) and continue to cook for a further minute.

4 Sprinkle the turmeric, cumin and seasoning over the vegetables and mix well. Add the crab meat and mussels and stir-fry for 1 minute.

5 Stir in the cooked rice and bean-sprouts and stir-fry for 2 minutes or until really hot and well mixed.

6 Adjust the seasoning and serve very hot, garnished with crab claws and mangetout (snow peas).

FRESH CRAB

To prepare fresh crab, first twist off the claws and legs. Crack with a heavy knife and pick out the meat with a skewer. Discard the gills and pull out the under shell; discard the stomach sac. Pull the soft meat from the shell. Cut open the body section and prise out the meat with a skewer. Use white meat only in this dish.

STEP 2

STEP 3

STEP 4

STEP 5

COCONUT RICE

A pale yellow rice flavoured with coconut and spices to serve as an accompaniment – or as a main dish with added diced chicken or pork.

SERVES 4

90 g/ 3 oz creamed coconut
750 ml/ 1¼ pints/ 3 cups boiling water
1 tbsp sunflower oil (or olive oil for a
    stronger flavour)
1 onion, thinly sliced or chopped
250 g/8 oz/generous 1 cup long-grain rice
¼ tsp turmeric
6 whole cloves
1 cinnamon stick
½ tsp salt
60-90 g/2-3 oz/½ cup raisins or sultanas
60 g/2 oz/½ cup walnut or pecan halves,
    roughly chopped
2 tbsp pumpkin seeds (optional)
watercress sprigs, to garnish (optional)

1 Blend the creamed coconut with half the boiling water until smooth, then mix in the remainder and stir until well blended.

2 Heat the oil in the wok, add the onion and stir-fry gently for 3-4 minutes until the onion begins to soften but not brown.

3 Rinse the rice thoroughly under cold running water, drain well and add to the wok with the turmeric. Cook for 1-2 minutes, stirring all the time.

4 Add the coconut milk, cloves, cinnamon stick and salt and bring to the boil. Cover with the wok lid, or a lid made of foil, and simmer very gently for 10 minutes.

5 Add the raisins, nuts and pumpkin seeds, if using, and mix well. Cover the wok again and continue to cook for a further 5-8 minutes or until all the liquid has been absorbed and the rice is tender.

6 Remove from the heat and leave to stand, still tightly covered, for 5 minutes before serving. Remove the cinnamon stick. Serve garnished with watercress sprigs, if liked.

VARIATION

250g/8oz/1 cup cooked chicken or pork cut into dice or thin slivers may be added with the raisins to turn this into a main dish. The addition of coconut milk makes the cooked rice slightly sticky.

FRIED RICE WITH PRAWNS (SHRIMP)

Use either large peeled prawns or tiger prawns (shrimp)
for this rice dish.

SERVES 4

300 g/10 oz/1¹/₂ cups long-grain rice
4 spring onions (scallions), thinly sliced
    diagonally
125 g/4 oz closed cup or button
    mushrooms, thinly sliced
1 x 200 g/7 oz can water chestnuts, drained
    and sliced
¹/₂ bunch of watercress, roughly chopped
2 eggs
4 tsp cold water
3 tbsp sunflower oil
1 garlic clove, crushed
2 tbsp oyster or anchovy sauce
250 g/8 oz peeled prawns (shrimp),
    defrosted if frozen
salt and pepper
watercress sprigs, to garnish (optional)

1 Cook the rice in boiling salted
water, following the instructions
given in Chinese Fried Rice (see page 56)
and keep warm.

2 Beat each egg separately with 2
teaspoons of cold water and salt
and pepper. Heat 2 teaspoons of oil in a
wok, swirling it around until really hot.
Pour in the first egg, swirl it around and
leave to cook undisturbed until set.
Remove to a plate or board and repeat

with the second egg. Cut the omelettes
into 2.5 cm/1 in squares.

3 Heat the remaining oil in the wok
and when really hot add the spring
onions (scallions) and garlic and stir-fry
for 1 minute. Add the mushrooms and
continue to cook for a further 2 minutes.

4 Stir in the oyster or anchovy sauce
and seasoning and add the water
chestnuts and prawns (shrimp); stir-fry
for 2 minutes.

5 Stir in the cooked rice and stir-fry
for 1 minute, then add the
watercress and omelette squares and stir-
fry for a further 1-2 minutes until piping
hot. Serve at once garnished with sprigs
of watercress, if liked.

PEELING PRAWNS (SHRIMP)

Pull off the head, then peel off the shell
from the body, leaving the tail intact. Make
a shallow cut along the back and remove
the dark intestinal vein.

STEP 1

STEP 2

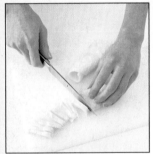

STEP 3

STEP 4

CHINESE FRIED RICE

The rice for this dish may be cooked in the wok or conventionally in a saucepan, but it is essential to use cold, dry rice with separate grains to make this recipe properly.

SERVES 4 (OR 6 AS AN ACCOMPANIMENT)

750 ml/1¼ pints/3 cups water
½ tsp salt
300 g/10 oz/1½ cups long-grain rice
2 eggs
4 tsp cold water
3 tbsp sunflower oil
4 spring onions (scallions), sliced diagonally
1 red, green or yellow (bell) pepper, cored, seeded and thinly sliced
3-4 lean rashers bacon, rinded and cut into strips
200 g/7 oz fresh bean-sprouts
125 g/4 oz frozen peas, defrosted
2 tbsp soy sauce (optional)
salt and pepper

1 Pour the water into the wok with the salt and bring to the boil. Rinse the rice in a sieve under cold water until the water runs clear, drain well and add to the boiling water. Stir well, then cover the wok tightly with the lid or a lid made of foil, and simmer gently for 12-13 minutes. (Don't remove the lid during cooking or the steam will escape and the rice will not be cooked.)

2 Remove the lid, give the rice a good stir and spread out on a large plate or baking sheet to cool and dry.

3 Beat each egg separately with salt and pepper and 2 teaspoons cold water. Heat 1 tablespoon of oil in the wok, swirling it around until really hot. Pour in the first egg, swirl it around and leave to cook undisturbed until set. Remove to a board or plate; repeat with the second egg. Cut the omelettes into thin slices.

4 Add the remaining oil to the wok and when really hot add the spring onions (scallions) and (bell) pepper and stir-fry for 1-2 minutes. Add the bacon and continue to stir-fry for a further 1-2 minutes. Add the bean-sprouts and peas and toss together thoroughly; stir in the soy sauce if using.

5 Add the rice and seasoning and stir-fry for a minute or so then add the strips of omelette and continue to stir for about 2 minutes or until the rice is piping hot. Serve at once.

COOKED RICE

If you have time, it is best to cook the rice earlier in the day, so that it is completely cold and dry before being added to the hot sauce in the wok.

CHAPTER FIVE

Meat & Poultry

Provided you use the best cuts of meat and poultry, you can cook
almost anything in the wok. Never try to cook cheap cuts of meat
by this method: the quick cooking simply will not do it justice,
and the result may be very tough. But if you choose steaks of beef,
pork, lamb and veal you cannot go far wrong; you can
also use fillets and in fact any good cut that can be successfully
grilled (broiled) or fried. The same applies to poultry
and game: use the breasts, and any other parts
which are free of gristle and sinew, bone and skin.

Cut the selected meat or poultry into strips 2.5-5 cm/1-2 in wide,
and then cut it thinly into strips, always across the grain of the
flesh. This exposes the maximum of cut surface: once the
meat is added to the hot oil in the wok it will seal
very quickly, thus keeping in the juices.

The cooking time is minimal, provided you stir-fry all the time once
the food is added to the well-heated wok. The shape of the wok
gives the maximum of heated surface, and with a good spatula
you can stir and toss the meat quickly until it is
evenly cooked. In some recipes the cooked meat is
removed while other ingredients are cooked and
then returned to the wok: make sure it is
well heated again before serving.

*Opposite: Coriander,
peppercorns, dried chillies, and
other spices traditionally used
when cooking in a wok.*

STEP 2

STEP 3

STEP 4

STEP 6

CHICKEN WITH PEANUT SAUCE

A tangy stir-fry with a strong peanut flavour. Serve with freshly boiled rice or noodles.

SERVES 4

4 boneless, skinned chicken breasts, about
    625 g/1¼ lb
4 tbsp soy sauce
4 tbsp sherry
3 tbsp crunchy peanut butter
2 tbsp sunflower oil
4-6 spring onions (scallions), thinly sliced
    diagonally
350 g/12 oz courgettes (zucchini), trimmed
1 x 250 g/8 oz can bamboo shoots, well
    drained and sliced
salt and pepper
4 tbsp desiccated (shredded) coconut, toasted

1 Cut the chicken into thin strips across the grain and season lightly with salt and pepper.

2 Stir the soy sauce in a bowl with the sherry and peanut butter until smooth and well blended.

3 Cut the courgettes (zucchini) into 5 cm/2 in lengths and then cut into sticks about 5mm/¼ in thick.

4 Heat the oil in the wok, swirling it around until it is really hot. Add the spring onions (scallions) and stir-fry for a minute or so then add the chicken

and stir-fry for 3-4 minutes until well sealed and almost cooked.

5 Add the courgettes (zucchini) and bamboo shoots and continue to stir-fry for 1-2 minutes.

6 Add the peanut butter mixture and heat thoroughly, stirring all the time so everything is coated in the sauce as it thickens. Adjust the seasoning and serve very hot, sprinkled with toasted coconut.

VARIATION

This dish can also be made with turkey fillet or pork fillet. For coconut lovers dissolve 30 g/1 oz creamed coconut in 2-3 tablespoons boiling water and add to the soy sauce mixture before adding to the wok

STEP 1

STEP 2

STEP 3

STEP 5

DUCK WITH LIME & KIWI FRUIT

Tender breasts of duck served in thin slices with a sweet but very tangy lime and wine sauce full of pieces of kiwi fruit.

SERVES 4

4 boneless or part-boned duck breasts
2 large limes
2 tbsp sunflower oil
4 spring onions (scallions), thinly sliced
    diagonally
125 g/4 oz carrots, cut into matchsticks
6 tbsp dry white wine
60 g/2 oz/¼ cup white sugar
2 kiwi fruit, peeled, halved and sliced
salt and pepper
parsley sprigs and lime halves in knots (see
    page 77) to garnish

1 Remove any excess fat from the duck, then prick the skin all over with a fork or skewer and lay in a shallow dish in a single layer. Remove the rind from the limes using a citrus zester or grate it coarsely. Squeeze the juice from the limes (there should be at least 3 tablespoons, if not make up with lemon juice), and add half the strips of lime and half the juice to the duck breasts, rubbing in thoroughly. Leave to stand in a cool place for at least 1 hour, turning the breasts at least once.

2 Drain the duck breasts thoroughly. Heat 1 tablespoon of oil in the wok, swirling it around until it is really hot.

Add the duck and fry quickly to seal all over then lower the heat a little and continue to cook for about 5 minutes, turning several times until just cooked through and well browned all over. Remove and keep warm.

3 Wipe the wok clean with paper towels and heat the remaining oil in it. Add the spring onions (scallions) and carrots and stir-fry for about 1 minute then add the remaining lime marinade, wine and sugar. Bring to the boil and simmer for 2-3 minutes until slightly syrupy.

4 Replace the duck breasts in the sauce, season well and add the kiwi fruit. Cook for about a minute or until really hot and both the duck and kiwi fruit are well coated in the sauce.

5 Cut each duck breast into slices, leaving a "hinge" at one end, open out into a fan shape and arrange on plates. Spoon the sauce over and around the duck, sprinkle with the remaining pieces of lime peel and garnish with parsley leaves and lime halves.

PORK BALLS WITH MINTED SAUCE

Made with lean minced pork the balls are first stir-fried, then braised in the wok with stock and pickled walnuts to give a tangy flavour.

SERVES 4

500 g/1 lb lean minced pork
45 g/1½ oz/¾ cup fine fresh white
   breadcrumbs
½ tsp ground allspice
1 garlic clove, crushed
2 tbsp freshly chopped mint
1 egg, beaten
2 tbsp sunflower oil
1 red (bell) pepper, cored, seeded and thinly
   sliced
250 ml/8 fl oz/1 cup chicken stock
4 pickled walnuts, sliced
salt and pepper
rice or Chinese noodles, to serve
fresh mint, to garnish

1 Combine the pork, breadcrumbs, seasoning, allspice, garlic and half the chopped mint in a bowl, then bind together with the egg. Shape the meat mixture into 20 small balls with your hands, damping your hands if it is easier for shaping.

2 Heat the oil in the wok, swirling it around until really hot, then stir-fry the pork balls until browned all over, about 4-5 minutes. Remove from the wok with a slotted spoon as they are ready and drain on paper towels.

3 Pour off all but 1 tablespoon of fat and oil from the wok then add the red (bell) pepper and stir-fry for 2-3 minutes, or until it is beginning to soften, but not colour.

4 Add the stock and bring to the boil. Season well and replace the pork balls, stirring well to coat in the sauce; simmer for 7-10 minutes, turning them from time to time.

5 Add the remaining chopped mint and the pickled walnuts to the wok and continue to simmer for 2-3 minutes, turning the pork balls regularly to coat them in the sauce.

6 Adjust the seasoning and serve with rice or Chinese noodles, or with a stir-fried vegetable dish, garnished with sprigs of fresh mint.

STEP 1

STEP 2

STEP 3

STEP 4

CHICKEN WITH CELERY & CASHEWS

Stir-fry yellow bean sauce, widely available bottled, gives this quick and easy Chinese dish a really authentic taste. Pecan nuts can be used in place of the cashews.

SERVES 4

3-4 boneless, skinned chicken breasts, about 625g/1¼ lb
2 tbsp sunflower or vegetable oil
125 g/4 oz/1 cup cashew nuts (unsalted)
4-6 spring onions (scallions), thinly sliced diagonally
5-6 celery sticks, thinly sliced diagonally
1 x 175 g/6 oz jar stir-fry yellow bean sauce
salt and pepper
celery leaves, to garnish (optional)

1 Cut the chicken into thin slices across the grain.

2 Heat the oil in the wok, swirling it around until really hot. Add the cashew nuts and stir-fry until they begin to brown, then add the chicken and stir-fry until well sealed and almost cooked through.

3 Add the spring onions (scallions) and celery and continue to stir-fry for 2–3 minutes, stirring the food well around the wok.

4 Add the stir-fry yellow bean sauce, season lightly and toss until the chicken and vegetables are thoroughly coated with the sauce and piping hot. Serve at once with plain boiled rice, garnished with celery leaves, if liked.

VARIATION

This recipe can be adapted to use turkey fillets or steaks, or pork fillet or boneless steaks. Cut the turkey or pork lengthwise first, then slice thinly across the grain. Alternatively, cut into 2 cm/¾ in cubes.

RED SPICED BEEF

A spicy stir-fry flavoured with paprika, chilli and tomato,
with a crisp bite to it from the celery strips.

SERVES 4

625 g/1¼ lb sirloin or rump steak
2 tbsp paprika
2-3 tsp mild chilli powder
½ tsp salt
6 celery sticks
4 tomatoes, peeled, seeded and sliced
6 tbsp stock or water
2 tbsp tomato purée (paste)
2 tbsp clear honey
3 tbsp wine vinegar
1 tbsp Worcestershire sauce
2 tbsp sunflower oil
4 spring onions (scallions), thinly sliced
 diagonally
1-2 garlic cloves, crushed
Chinese noodles, to serve
celery leaves, to garnish (optional)

1 Cut the steak across the grain into narrow strips 1cm/½in thick and place in a bowl. Combine the paprika, chilli powder and salt, add to the beef and mix thoroughly until the meat strips are evenly coated with the spices. Leave the beef to marinate in a cool place for at least 30 minutes.

2 Cut the celery into 5 cm/2 in lengths, then cut the lengths into strips about 5 mm/¼ in thick.

3 Combine the stock, tomato purée (paste), honey, vinegar and Worcestershire sauce.

4 Heat the oil in the wok, swirling it around until really hot. Add the spring onion (scallions), celery and garlic and stir-fry for about 1 minute until the vegetables are beginning to soften, then add the steak strips. Stir-fry over a high heat for 3-4 minutes until the meat is well sealed.

5 Add the sauce to the wok and continue to stir-fry briskly until thoroughly coated and sizzling.

6 Serve with noodles and garnish with celery leaves, if liked.

VARIATION

To give the beef a hotter taste, use hot chilli powder instead of the mild, or add 1 teaspoon hot chilli sauce.

SUKIYAKI BEEF

An easy way of giving beef a Japanese flavour is to marinate the meat in teriyaki sauce and sherry: it can be left for anything from 1-24 hours. Hearts of palm and mushrooms blend well with the beef.

STEP 2

STEP 3

STEP 4

STEP 5

SERVES 4

2.5 cm/1 in ginger root, grated
1 garlic clove, crushed
4 tbsp sherry
4 tbsp teriyaki sauce
500-625 g/1-1¼ lb sirloin, rump or
 fillet steak
125 g/4 oz button or closed cup
 mushrooms, thinly sliced
1 x 425 g/15 oz can hearts of palm
2 tbsp sesame or sunflower oil
salt and pepper

TO GARNISH:
sesame seeds (optional)
spring onion (scallion) tassles

1 Blend the ginger in a shallow dish with the garlic, sherry and teriyaki sauce, adding a little salt.

2 Cut the steak into narrow strips about 2.5-4 cm/1-1½ in long, across the grain. Add the strips to the marinade in the dish, mix thoroughly to coat, cover and leave in a cool place for at least 1 hour and up to 24 hours.

3 Drain the hearts of palm and cut into slanting slices about 1 cm/½ in thick.

4 Remove the beef from the marinade with a slotted spoon, reserving the marinade. Heat the oil in the wok, swirling it around until really hot. Add the beef and stir-fry for 2 minutes, then add the mushrooms and continue to cook for a further minute.

5 Add the hearts of palm to the wok with the reserved marinade and stir-fry for another minute, making sure the meat is thoroughly coated in the sauce. Adjust the seasoning and serve sprinkled with sesame seeds (if using) and garnished with spring onion (scallion) tassles.

SPRING ONION (SCALLION) TASSLES

To make tassles, first trim the spring onions (scallions) into short lengths, about 5 cm (2 in). Using a sharp knife, slice lengthways, leaving about 2.5 cm (1 in) white root at the end. Place the tassles in a bowl of cold water for about an hour, until they curl up.

BEEF WITH BEANS

Strips of steak with a strong flavouring of sherry, teriyaki sauce and orange make an ideal dish for entertaining.

STEP 1

SERVES 4

500-625 g/1-1¼ lb sirloin, rump or fillet steak
1 orange
2 tbsp sesame oil
4 spring onions (scallions), thinly sliced diagonally
175 g/6 oz French or fine beans, cut into 2-3 pieces
1 garlic clove, crushed
4 tbsp sherry
1½ tbsp teriyaki sauce
¼ tsp ground allspice
1 tsp sugar
1 x 425 g/15 oz can cannellini beans, drained
salt and pepper

TO GARNISH:
canelled orange slices (see right)
fresh bay leaves

1 Cut the steak into narrow strips, about 4 cm/1½ in long, cutting across the grain.

2 Remove the peel from the orange using a citrus zester, or pare thinly with a potato peeler, and cut the rind into julienne strips. Squeeze the orange and reserve the juice.

3 Heat 1 tablespoon of the oil in the wok, swirling it around until really hot. Add the strips of beef and stir-fry briskly for about 2 minutes, then remove from the wok and keep warm.

4 Add the remaining oil to the wok and when hot add the spring onions (scallions) and garlic and stir-fry for 1-2 minutes. Add the French beans and continue to cook for 2 minutes.

5 Add the sherry, teriyaki, orange rind and 3 tablespoons of orange juice, allspice, sugar and seasoning and when well mixed return the beef and any juices to the wok.

6 Stir-fry for 1-2 minutes then add the cannellini beans and stir until piping hot. Adjust the seasoning. Serve garnished with canelled orange twists and bay leaves.

CANELLED ORANGE

Using a canelle knife make evenly spaced grooves all around an orange from stem to base. Cut the fruit into slices approx 5 mm/¼ in thick and then into quarters.

STEP 2

STEP 3

STEP 5

STEP 1

STEP 2

STEP 3

STEP 4

FIVE-SPICE LAMB

Chinese five-spice powder is a blend of cinnamon, fennel, star anise, ginger and cloves, all finely ground together. It gives an authentic Chinese flavour to meat and poultry dishes.

SERVES 4

625 g/1¼ lb lean boneless lamb (leg or fillet)
2 tsp Chinese five-spice powder
3 tbsp sunflower oil
1 red (bell) pepper, cored, seeded and thinly sliced
1 green (bell) pepper, cored, seeded and thinly sliced
1 yellow or orange (bell) pepper, cored, seeded and thinly sliced
4-6 spring onions (scallions), thinly sliced diagonally
175 g/6 oz French or fine beans, cut into 4 cm/1½ in lengths
2 tbsp soy sauce
4 tbsp sherry
salt and pepper
Chinese noodles, to serve

TO GARNISH:
strips of red and yellow (bell) pepper
fresh coriander leaves

1 Cut the lamb into narrow strips, about 4 cm/1½ in long, across the grain. Place in a bowl, add the five-spice powder and ¼ teaspoon salt, mix well and leave to marinate, covered, in a cool place for at least an hour and up to 24 hours.

2 Heat half the oil in the wok, swirling it around until really hot. Add the lamb and stir-fry briskly for 3-4 minutes until almost cooked through; remove from the pan.

3 Add the remaining oil to the wok and when hot add the (bell) peppers and spring onions (scallions). Stir-fry for 2-3 minutes, then add the beans and stir for a minute or so.

4 Add the soy sauce and sherry to the wok and when hot replace the lamb and any juices. Stir-fry for 1-2 minutes until the lamb is really hot again and thoroughly coated in the sauce. Season to taste.

5 Serve with Chinese noodles, garnished with strips of red and green (bell) pepper and fresh coriander.

FIVE-SPICE POWDER

Chinese five-spice powder has an unmistakable flavour. Use it sparingly, as it is very pungent.

THE WOK

SAUCES

Soy sauce

This is widely used in all Eastern cookery and is made from fermented yellow soya beans mixed with wheat, salt, yeast and sugar. It comes in both light and dark varieties (with extra caramel for colour). There are many brands and some tend to be rather salty, particularly the light ones; the darker soy sauce tends to be sweeter and is more often used in dips and sauces rather than in the actual cooking.

Oyster sauce

Made from fermented oysters and fish to give a thick dark sauce with a strong flavour. It is widely used in beef stir-fries.

Teriyaki sauce

This gives an authentic Japanese flavouring to stir-fries using chicken, beef, pork and vegetables. Thick and dark brown, it contains soy sauce, vinegar, sesame oil and spices as main ingredients.

Bean sauces

Black bean and yellow bean sauces add an instant authentic Chinese flavour to stir-fries. Black bean is the stronger and used more often with beef and other meats but can be used with poultry and vegetables; the yellow bean variety is milder and excellent with chicken, vegetables and even fish.

The wok is an ancient Chinese invention, the name coming from the Cantonese, meaning a cooking vessel. The exact date of its appearance is unknown, but it has been used in the East for many centuries, and probably began life as a simple cooking utensil in farm kitchens, where speedy cooking was essential. The results were so good and the wok was so versatile, needing only a small amount of heat, that its popularity grew. Gradually everyone began to use one, from farm workers to palace chefs, and it became the classic cooking utensil it is today.

The clever design of a wok makes it easy to use with such versatility: as well as stir-frying, it is also excellent for steaming, braising and deep-frying. The unique shaped pan, like a frying pan but with a spherical base and high sloping sides, heats first from the base and then up the sides, enabling the food to be tossed over a high heat so that it cooks both quickly and evenly. It is essential to heat the wok sufficiently before adding the food to ensure this quick and even cooking.

Healthy eating

Wok cooking is a very healthy way of eating, as you need only the minimum amount of oil to cook with, swirling it around the wok. And because only top-quality lean meat, poultry and other ingredients are used, generally the cholesterol and fat levels are kept low, which in turn keeps down the calorie intake too.

CHOOSING YOUR WOK

There are several types of Chinese wok on the market, most of which are very reasonably priced. Although a heavy-based frying pan can be used for stir-frying, it certainly doesn't conduct the heat in the same way as a wok, nor is it as easy to toss the food without the unique wok shape . Some woks now have a flatter base than the original spherical ones (which were used to cook over an open fire, balanced on a specially shaped metal ring) to adapt to cooking on a conventional hob.

Materials

Choose a simple wok made of carbon steel, widely available from oriental supermarkets and kitchen equipment shops, for the best results; or try one of the modern non-stick woks which also give good results; but be wary of stainless steel varieties because they are not such good heat conductors. There are also electric woks available, but they are expensive and it is not easy to alter the heat quickly during cooking.

The handle or handles should be made of wood or solid plastic; metal ones get too hot to touch and can cause burnt fingers. It also needs a lid for steaming and to hold in the heat for braising and other cooking. If you buy a wok in a set, it will come with a lid and several other accessories such as stands and cooking utensils but sometimes these are more expensive than buying the extra items separately.

Some woks come with one handle, known as a pau wok, and this is best for stir-frying as one hand can hold the handle whilst the other hand holds the spatula and stirs. The two-handled varieties are known as Cantonese woks and are good for steaming and deep-frying as they usually have a flatter base.

Caring for your wok

Authentic Chinese steel or cast-iron woks need constant care after each use or they will become rusty; but if looked after they will last for years, never wearing out. If the wok is bought from an oriental store it will probably come coated in oil as protection and this should be removed before use with hot water and detergent and then carefully dried. Next the new wok will need to be "seasoned" before use. Place over a low heat and heat until really hot all over, then remove from the heat. Add a little oil to the wok and swirl and brush it all around the inside, and then rub all over the inside of the wok with paper towels until the paper is black. Continue to rub with fresh paper towels dipped in oil until the paper no longer turns black. The wok is then ready for use. If you have a non-stick wok, it is not necessary to season it, but always follow the maker's instructions before you use it for the first time.

Each time you finish using the wok it must be washed in hot water and then dried very thoroughly. Before putting it away rub with a light layer of oil on a pad of paper towels. If it still goes rusty don't worry, simply scrub off the rust with a scourer and when clean repeat the seasoning process before use.

ACCESSORIES FOR YOUR WOK

Spatula First you need a spatula for stirring the food around in the wok; this can be of wood, plastic or metal, but avoid metal if using a non-stick wok as it will damage the surface. Wooden chopsticks can also be used for stirring.

A perforated spoon is required for removing pieces of cooked food from stock or sauces or when deep-frying.

Drainer This is a wire inset which covers nearly half the wok and which can be hooked over the edge to use as a drainer or to keep cooked food warm.

Steamer If you intend to steam foods in your wok you will need a bamboo steamer. They come in assorted sizes and with two or three layers and a lid. The base of each layer is made up of woven bamboo which allows the steam through during cooking. The steaming basket is placed in the wok on a trivet with a little water in the wok, and then the whole thing is covered with the lid.

PREPARING FOOD FOR THE WOK

Everything should be prepared before you actually start to cook or the first ingredients will be overcooked before the others are ready to add.

Remember that the food must always be of the highest quality: stir-frying is certainly not the cheapest method of cooking, but it is one of the most tasty and easy to prepare. Use meat suitable for grilling or pan-frying, not the cuts that

CHILLIES

These come both fresh and dried and in colours from green through yellow, orange and red to almost brown. The 'hotness' varies enormously so always use with caution, but as a guide the smaller they are the hotter they will be. The seeds are the hottest part and more often discarded. Take care when cutting chillies with bare hands not to touch your eyes: the juices will cause awful irritation and stinging, so wash hands very thoroughly.

Chilli powders should also be used sparingly and check whether it is pure chilli or a chilli seasoning or blend which should be milder. Chilli sauces are also widely used in this type of cookery but again they vary in strength from hot to exceedingly hot and also in sweetness – some being both very hot and very sharp!

LIME GARNISH

Cut the limes in half crosswise and then trim a piece off the base so they stand upright. Using a small, sharp knife, pare off a thin strip of rind from the top of the lime halves, about 5 mm/¼ in thick, but do not detach it. Tie the strip into a knot with the end bending over the cut surface of the lime.

SPECIAL INGREDIENTS

Bamboo shoots

These come in cans, are usually ready sliced and are very bland in flavour but easily absorb other flavours during cooking. They are shoots which come from the base of the bamboo plants, are parboiled and canned ready for use. Widely available in supermarkets.

Water chestnuts

Again available in cans, they are small peeled crisp white bulbs, which are usually sliced before adding to a recipe. They are bland in flavour but they always stay crisp so add special texture to a dish.

Creamed coconut

This comes in a block and is diluted with boiling water to make a coconut milk which can be added immediately to curries, casseroles, stir -fries and sauces. It is made from fresh coconut and is much easier to use than grated fresh coconut or dessicated coconut, both of which need steeping in boiling water and careful straining before use.

Five-spice powder

A unique blend of ground spices to give a highly aromatic flavouring with a hint of liquorice. It includes star anise, cinnamon, cloves, fennel and Szechuan pepper.

are only suitable for casseroles. This is because the food must cook in the shortest time possible; stir-frying will make the best of good quality food, but it cannot improve inferior ingredients.

Always read the whole recipe before you start, and make sure everything is prepared and all ingredients are to hand. Preparation always takes much longer than the actual cooking time when you use a wok. If you are entertaining, all the preparation can be done earlier in the day, with only the final cooking left to be done at the last minute.

Although oriental cooks tend to use a variety of cleavers for chopping, a good sharp kitchen knife and chopping board will do just as well. All ingredients should be cut into uniform sizes and shapes with as many cut surfaces exposed as possible, hence cutting on the slant or diagonal, or into julienne strips or matchsticks. Meat and poultry should be cut into narrow strips across the grain, which enables it to be sealed quickly, thus keeping in the juices and giving tender results.

COOKING TECHNIQUES

Stir-frying

This is the most popular method of cooking in a wok. Once the food has been prepared and you are ready to begin cooking, add the oil to the wok and heat it, swirling it round until it is really hot. If it is sufficiently hot the ingredients added should not stick at all but sizzle and immediately begin to cook.

Most recipes begin by cooking the onions, garlic and ginger, because they help to flavour the oil. The heat may

need to be lowered a little at first but must be increased again as the other ingredients are added. Gas probably gives the best results because of the speed of controlling the heat, and the fact that the curved base of the wok fits so well into the hob. Electricity and solid fuel hobs are more efficient if a flat-based wok is used.

Sometimes the first ingredients need to be removed from the wok and kept warm while cooking the remainder or making the sauce, but do everything speedily and when all the ingredients are back in the wok, stir thoroughly together and be sure they are piping hot before serving. Always add the ingredients in the order they are listed in the recipe. While the food is cooking, keep stirring. When you add a sauce or liquid at the end of a recipe, first push the cooked food to the side of the wok, so the sauce heats as quickly as possible, then toss the food back into the sauce over a high heat so it boils rapidly and thickens the sauce. Once cooked, serve as soon as possible.

Deep-frying

The Cantonese wok with its slightly flattened base and two handles is best for deep-frying and it requires less oil than a conventional deep fat fryer. It is usually used for frying battered or egg and crumbed morsels of food or parcels of food encased in pastry. The best oil to use is something like groundnut, which has a high smoke point and mild flavour, so it will neither burn nor taste the food.

If you have a round-based wok use a metal wok stand to keep it stable during cooking (some wok sets include a stand). The semi-circular rack which clips onto the side of the wok is a great help for both draining food and keeping things warm when cooked. As food drains the excess oil simply drips back into the wok. It is not necessary to preheat the wok. Simply add the oil (approx 600 ml/1 pint should be sufficient) and heat until the required temperature is reached: use a thermometer or test until it takes 30 seconds to brown a cube of bread.

The cooking time is determined by the size of the ingredients to be cooked, and it is essential that the oil is hot enough to seal the batter or pastry as quickly as possible without the food absorbing any more oil than necessary. When golden brown, remove with a slotted spoon and drain first on the special drainer attached to the wok and then transfer to paper towels to remove any further oil. Serve at once.

Take care that the pieces of food to be deep-fried are as dry as possible before adding to the hot oil in the wok to prevent splattering and splashing.

Steaming

This is a particularly good method for cooking fish, seafood, poultry and vegetables. You need a large wok and a bamboo steamer with a lid. The wok needs a little water in the bottom but it must not reach the base of the bamboo steamer when it is in position: stand the steamer on a trivet. Put the food on a plate that will just fit into the steamer and place it carefully in one of the layers. Seasonings, herbs and flavourings may be added, then put on the lid and steam until tender (following the times given in the recipes). It is very important to keep the lid on so no steam can escape. Make sure the wok does not boil dry – add extra boiling water as necessary. The main advantage of cooking by this method is that there is no fat required and so it is particularly healthy.

The steamer has several layers, which can be stacked on top of each other so more than one type of food can be cooked at the same time, e.g., fish or strips of chicken and two different vegetables.

If you don't have a bamboo steamer, you can still steam food in the wok. Simply put a plate on a metal or wooden trivet in the wok with water to just below the plate and cover with a lid.

Braising/Simmering

The wok can also be used as a large saucepan and is excellent for making stir-fry soups for example. Simply stir-fry the ingredients in a little oil, add the liquid, seasonings and flavourings and simmer either uncovered or with a lid. With this type of soup the vegetables should still have a good "bite" to them, so the cooking time is a lot less than with traditional soups.

Pan-frying and braising are speeded up using a wok because of the extra heat distribution. Simply fry the ingredients quickly so they are well sealed to keep the juices in, then add the stock or sauce, cover and simmer gently until tender. Sometimes it is better not to cover the wok so that the cooking liquid is reduced, which intensifies the flavours even more. Whichever method is used stir from time to time to prevent any possible sticking, and to ensure the ingredients are evenly cooked.

Sesame oil and seeds
This oil is made from pressed roasted sesame seeds to give a highly aromatic oil. It has a low smoke point so should be combined with a groundnut or sunflower oil for stir-frying; or simply drizzle over cooked food before serving. The darker the colour, the stronger the flavour. The seeds are used to add flavour and texture to many dishes. If dry-fried or toasted first the flavour is accentuated. They are rich in B vitamins and high in protein and calcium so make a very healthy addition.

Bean curd (tofu)
This is a highly nutritious food made from soya beans, white in colour and with the texture of soft cheese. It is high in protein yet low in fat and a great favourite with vegetarians. It can be cut into pieces which keep their shape during cooking. For sauces and dips buy the silken tofu, which is like a thick yogurt; both varieties are widely available in health food shops and large supermarkets.

Ginger root
Peel it carefully and then either grate, chop finely or cut into thin slivers and use as a seasoning. Widely available in supermarkets, it will keep for a couple of weeks or so in a cool dry place. Crystallized and preserved ginger are not good substitutes and are best used in sweet or uncooked salad dishes.

INDEX